SELECTED CASES ON THE LAW OF SHOPLIFTING

SELECTED CASES ON THE LAW OF SHOPLIFTING

By

SHERMAN E. FEIN, J.D., Ed.D.

and

ARTHUR M. MASKELL, J.D.

With a Foreword by
Warren E. McAvoy

Director of Security
Food Marts, Inc.
Holyoke, Massachusetts

CHARLES   C   THOMAS   •   PUBLISHER
Springfield • Illinois • U.S.A.

Published and Distributed Throughout the World by
CHARLES C THOMAS ● PUBLISHER
Bannerstone House
301-327 East Lawrence Avenue, Springfield, Illinois, U.S.A.

© *1975, by* CHARLES C THOMAS ● PUBLISHER
ISBN 0-398-03354-4 (cloth)
ISBN 0-398-03355-2 (paper)
Library of Congress Catalog Card Number: 74-32139

With THOMAS BOOKS *careful attention is given to all details of
manufacturing and design. It is the Publisher's desire to present books that are
satisfactory as to their physical qualities and artistic possibilities and
appropriate for their particular use.* THOMAS BOOKS *will be true to those
laws of quality that assure a good name and good will.*

Printed in the United States of America
R-1

Library of Congress Cataloging in Publication Data

Fein, Sherman E
    Selected cases on the law of shoplifting.

    Includes index.
    1. Shoplifting--United States--Cases. I. Maskell,
Arthur M., joint author. II. Title.
KF9352.A7F4   345′.73′0262   74-32139
ISBN 0-398-03354-4
ISBN 0-398-03355-2 pbk.

FOREWORD

SECURITY personnel, like all mortals, come in a
variety of shapes and sizes, and bring to their profession varying
degrees of competence and expertise.

When it comes to matters of the law, however, security men, be
they store detectives, store managers, or even security directors are
not experts, nor are they expected to be.

An awareness of the eventual consequences of their actions and
investigations in a court of law is obviously both essential and
desirable.

In compiling these cases which show the actual results in a
number of alleged shoplifting incidents Dr. Fein and Mr. Maskell
have, in my opinion, made a valuable contribution to the
education of all security and store personnel.

WARREN E. McAVOY

PREFACE

SELECTED CASES ON THE LAW OF SHOPLIFTING

FOR the businessman faced with the awesome upward spiral of labor and product costs, increased competition and governmental efforts to control prices, shoplifting has reached disaster proportions.

The prestigious *National Observer*, on January 4, 1971, in an article entitled, "Shoplifting Boom", quotes Howard Haimourtz of the National Retail Merchants Association as saying, "The total loss is about $3 billion a year." The same article cites a Federal Bureau of Investigation report which states that from 1960 through 1969, shoplifting increased 174 percent and the then FBI Director, J. Edgar Hoover, characterized this particular crime as the fastest growing larceny violation in the nation.

While these statistics are frightening to contemplate, the full impact of shoplifting becomes more meaningful when viewed from the perspective of its actual effect at the retail level.

According to a *Life Magazine* article entitled, "One Out of Sixty Is A Shoplifter," retailers who operate on low profit margins, often must ring up $30.00 in sales to break even after a $1.00 theft. The net effect for one 474 outlet chain, John's Bargain Stores, was to be driven into bankruptcy when pilferage reached a reported 10 percent of sales.

There can be little doubt that the ability, on the part of business, to control this horrendous pilferage problem can spell the difference between success and failure when reaching the bottom line on the balance sheet.

Responding to the obvious need, the Legislature of the Commonwealth of Massachusetts, in 1958, passed a law which, at least, makes it easier for merchants to apprehend shoplifters without the haunting fear of being faced with a counter action for false arrest. This particular statute reads as follows:

> In an action for false arrest or false imprisonment brought by any person by reason of having been detained for questioning on or in the immediate vicinity of the premises of a merchant, if such person was detained in a reasonable manner and for not more than a reasonable length of time by a person authorized to make arrests or by the merchant or his agent or servant authorized for such purpose and if there were reasonable grounds to believe that the person so detained was committing or attempting to commit larceny of goods for sale on such premises, it shall be a defense to such action. If such goods had not been purchased, and were concealed on or amongst the belongings of a person so detained, it shall be presumed that there were reasonable grounds for such belief. (Massachusetts General Laws, Chapter 231 — Section 94B)

While laws such as this do offer some relief, it is nonetheless true that each case which comes to court is decided on its own merits and according to its own particular set of facts.

The purpose of this book is to present actual cases which have been decided by various courts across the country. Hopefully, these decisions will give store owners, managers and security personnel some idea of the parameters within which they can gauge their actions in matters of shoplifting and pilferage.

Doctor SHERMAN E. FEIN
Doctor ARTHUR M. MASKELL

CONTENTS

SELECTED CASES
ON THE LAW OF
SHOPLIFTING

PROLOGUE

TEXT MATERIAL AND DEFINITIONS

THE cases contained herein were chosen to illustrate the problems that arise in various actions arising from shoplifting cases in a court of law. A review of these problems is helpful before reading the actual material presented.

A most important problem that should be recognized is that conflicting testimony is almost always presented to the court or jury hearing the case. The actual sequence of events then becomes a question of fact and depends entirely on which body of testimony the court or jury decides to choose as the accurate one. Therefore, intelligent personnel should be used for interviews with customers, and conversations should be well documented immediately after the interview.

Another important rule to follow is to enforce the rules already in existence. In case after case, problems arose because rules specifically created to avoid that particular problem were not enforced. A striking example in the selected cases is the self-service type retail outlet which checks incoming packages. In almost every case a customer was shopping in the store with some kind of article already on his person.

Every store management team should have a specific set of instructions and these instructions should be taught and reiterated on a regular basis. Otherwise the actual store procedure becomes something entirely different from that intended.

There are several suggestions that could be made that should be cardinal rules of conduct. If they are followed unswervingly, most problems will not arise.

The first and most important is that physical force should never be used. As can be seen from the selected cases, even a slight touching of another person can be considered battery by the court, and even a verbal threat is an assault.

An accusation of criminal conduct should not be made at any time. It is possible to investigate a suspected theft without accusing the suspect. This problem arises mostly from a question by the suspect such as "Do you think I'm a thief?". The wrong reply, such as "Yes, you stole something from the store" invites a suit. It becomes slander when voiced in front of witnesses. It is possible to reply without accusing, such as "You may have an article that wasn't checked out."

A third rule is to conduct all interviews out of the hearing of other customers. Most witnesses react adversely to authority and therefore become unfriendly witnesses. Not to mention the fact that a necessary element to the civil action for slander is that some member of the community hear the slanderous utterance.

A referral of findings to the proper authorities at the earliest possible moment serves two important purposes. False imprisonment requires an unnecessary detention of a person against his will. When an investigation is complete, the necessity to detain someone then ends unless further action is to be taken.

Also, the police are the proper source of any further action. If they feel there is reasonable cause for arrest, it is their responsibility to act. The store then avoids the possibility of a charge of malicious prosecution or false arrest. The decision is made by an experienced professional.

The value in reading these cases is not necessarily to discover new methods to avert legal problems. Most of these methods have been in existence for some time and their value well known.

It is rather to observe the end result of many situations the reader has been a part of at different times. Few management personnel follow a case through to a trial and verdict. The reason for specific rules and the result when they are violated are intended to be illustrated here. To proceed to court and win a verdict is not necessarily a victory, especially when trial expense and publicity are considered. The objective should be to avoid the necessity of litigation through effective and constant management techniques. A list of civil actions usually result from shoplifting cases and their definitions.

It should be noted that the following definitions may vary somewhat from state to state, but the broad interpretation is generally accepted.

FALSE IMPRISONMENT. This civil action is simply defined as illegal restraint of a person against his will. Any exercise of force, or express or implied threat of force by which, in fact, a person is deprived of his liberty, or is compelled to remain where he does not wish to remain, or go where he does not wish to go, is defined as "imprisonment." False imprisonment may be committed by words alone, or by acts alone, or both together.

It is not necessary that the individual be confined or even touched. The essence of the action is the restraint of the person. Therefore, he must feel he is being restrained by force or fear of force.

It is important to remember that consent by the individual is a defense to the action.

FALSE ARREST. Any unlawful physical restraint of another's liberty. This definition closely relates to the definition of false imprisonment and, therefore, the actions are very often seen together. Each state has a statute concerning what constitutes a legal arrest, and these statutory rules vary considerably from one state to another. In most states an arrest without a warrant is a very limited privilege, even when a police officer is involved. Most statutes allow a police officer and a private citizen to arrest without a warrant for a misdemeanor or minor public offense when the crime is committed or attempted in his presence. The arrest becomes unlawful when it is not authorized by statute.

MALICIOUS PROSECUTION. An action instituted with malice, or the specific intent to injure the defendant knowing there is no proper basis for the charge. There are four necessary elements that must be proved in order to sustain this action. The first is that a criminal proceeding was instituted by the defendant against the plaintiff. This requirement is not met by simply showing a report was made. If the police, making their own investigation and judgment, decide to bring a charge, this element is not proven.

The second requirement is that the proceedings terminate in favor of the accused; in other words, a not guilty verdict or dismissal of charges.

Thirdly, absence of probable cause to initiate the proceeding must be proven. Probable cause can be defined as what a reasonable man would consider reasonable under the circumstances to justify a charge being brought.

The fourth requirement is that malice be proven, or in the alternative that the primary purpose in instituting the proceedings is other than that of bringing an offender to justice.

LIBEL; SLANDER. Slander is the speaking of base and defamatory words which may prejudice another's reputation or means of livelihood. It is necessary that the words be spoken in front of another and loud enough so that other persons can hear them. This is because no damage to a reputation results if another person does not hear the malicious words.

Libel consists of slanderous words that are in print rather than spoken.

ASSAULT. An assault is an intentional offer of force to do another injury, under circumstances that create a fear of peril in the person assaulted. Therefore, an assault can occur without even touching the individual. Merely shaking a fist at someone and using threatening words can constitute an assault. If the blow is actually struck, then a battery has taken place. Battery is the inflicted injury.

CHARLOTTE ABNER v.
W. T. GRANT COMPANY

COURT OF APPEALS OF GEORGIA

October 16, 1964

ON April 20, 1963, Mrs. Abner entered the W. T. Grant Co. Store to do some shopping. She was accompanied by her two aunts. They spent a total of about fifteen minutes in the store.

While in the store they examined some handbags that were for sale, and one of Mrs. Abner's companions picked up a handbag and examined it. No one carried a handbag from the area. They left the store.

Mrs. Abner testified that she was about five feet out of the store, and on the public sidewalk, when she was "tapped" on the shoulder by a store employee. She agreed that the tapping was merely to attract her attention, and that she was not touched again.

The employee then asked her if she had purchased anything in the store. She replied that she had not. The store's agent said "What about that bag in your hand," and pointed at her handbag.

Mrs. Abner held her handbag up and said "This is mine." The store employee did not respond, but continued to look at the handbag. Mrs. Abner opened her handbag and said "See." It contained her items.

Mrs. Abner testified that the employee then gave her a "dirty look" and walked away. He did not say she could not leave.

Based on the sequence of events, Mrs. Abner brought an action for false imprisonment and slander against the store. It is worth quoting some of the allegations made by Mrs. Abner in her complaint.

Her complaint states that the store employee "with force of arms wantonly and willfully laid hold of the plaintiff" and

7

stopped her as she left the store. "He accused plaintiff of having stolen goods in her possession" and "having taken articles without paying for them." Also that "Plaintiff was restrained from leaving the front of the store and her pocketbook was searched."

The court dismissed both of Mrs. Abner's complaints after hearing her own testimony. As to the complaint for slander, the court stated that merely asking if an article was bought in the store is not an insulting statement.

In deciding on the charge of false imprisonment, the court stated a general definition of this term. It is the detention of another person unlawful. The cause of the restraint may be acts, words, or gestures which induce a feeling of apprehension that if one did not comply, force would be used.

Here Mrs. Abner's own testimony showed that no acts or words were used that might induce a fear of physical restraint.

MRS. ESTELLE BACHARACH v.
F. W. WOOLWORTH COMPANY

COURT OF APPEAL OF LOUISIANA

February 3, 1964

On August 16, 1958 Mrs. Bacharach was a customer in Woolworths, a self-service store. Another customer informed the manager that Mrs. Bacharach had secreted some merchandise in her handbag. The manager went to the customer who was at that time in the stationery department. He asked her to use a shopping basket furnished by the store to carry merchandise purchased, but she refused.

He noted that her handbag was made out of plastic and was clear enough so that one could see into it. He saw several articles similar to those on sale in the store. He left her then but continued to watch her.

About ten minutes later she went through the checkout counter and paid for her purchases. The manager then stopped her again.

Mrs. Bacharach testified that "He asked me if I had paid for all the merchandise and I told him, 'Yes, I paid for everything.' He said 'Are you sure you paid for all your merchandise?' I said 'Yes sir, I am.' He said 'Wouldn't you like to pay for the merchandise that you have in your handbag?' "

Mrs. Bacharach then dumped the contents of her handbag on the counter and the manager looked through it. He apologized at once on finding nothing belonging to the store.

About thirty or forty customers witnessed this incident as well as some relatives of Mrs. Bacharach. She testified she was mortified and was so nervous she could not drive her car. She was confined to bed for a week after the incident.

Mrs. Bacharach brought an action for slander and the court

9

found for her in the amount of $500.00. The manager's actions were slanderous. Although he never overtly accused her of theft, he implied it in actions and statements. Moreover, he had no reasonable cause to accuse her. The word of a stranger, a customer, is not sufficient evidence to make an accusation.

Even if it were a reasonable cause to suspect the customer, a public accusation reflecting on Mrs. Bacharach's honesty was unnecessary.

He could have questioned her without bringing it to the attention of others. Further, his apology does not release his bad conduct.

ALEX BANKS v. FOOD TOWN, INC.

COURT OF APPEAL OF LOUISIANA

November 19, 1957

MR. Banks brought an action against Food Town, Inc. for an unlawful search of his person. At the trial, Banks and the store employees gave conflicting testimony as to the sequence of events.

Harelson, a store employee, said Banks aroused his suspicions when he saw him make a motion to stick a "small object" with "a little color to it" under his shirt. Harelson testified that he did not see Banks take anything from the shelves. He saw Banks stop at a counter for a moment then walk hurriedly out of the store.

Harelson testified that he followed Banks outside the store and yelled to him, "Hey Fellow!" Banks stopped, turned around, threw up his hands and said "Search me." Harelson searched him, found nothing and did not detain him any longer.

Banks gave a different version of the incident. He said he went into the store to price beef, that he made no purchase. While there Harelson shouted to him "Hey you, come here, what do you have under your shirt?" Banks then testified that Harelson searched him without his permission and in front of several witnesses, inside the store.

Banks' contention is that he was unlawfully searched and that since it took place in front of witnesses, his reputation was damaged.

A store owner has the right to detain a customer whom he reasonably suspects of shoplifting. Probable cause for suspicion must be present.

In coming to a conclusion on the question of whether or not there was probable cause, the court chose to believe the testimony

11

of the store employees rather than Banks. That version being that Harelson saw Banks make a motion to stick something under his shirt, and that Banks agreed to the search.

Even though the court accepted the store employee's version, it found that there was no probable cause to search or detain Banks. It stressed that a customer has the right to enter a store and "window shop." The customer also has the right to place his hand in his pocket or under his shirt, and to walk at a fast pace. Something more than surmise is necessary to show probable cause. No one here testified to actually seeing Banks take anything.

In this situation the court would find the store at fault if the charge proves incorrect.

However, though no probable cause was found present, the court found for the store because testimony showed Banks had consented to be detained momentarily and searched.

BETTY JO ALLEN BLACK v.
CLARK'S GREENSBORO, INC.

SUPREME COURT OF NORTH CAROLINA

December 16, 1964

THE customer in this case brings an action for false imprisonment. Her allegation is that she suffered great mental anguish, embarrassment and humiliation when she was detained against her will for five minutes by the store employees.

The following are the facts which are taken as undisputed between the parties. On December 5, 1962 Betty Black, with two companions, went shopping at Clark's in Greensboro. They selected and paid for several items of merchandise. They left the store and got in their car in the parking lot.

There, two men, one showing a badge, asked her to open her pocketbook. She gave the pocketbook to one of the men who opened it and returned it to her. He asked to see a bracelet which was in the pocketbook. She gave it to him, and he examined it. He asked where she purchased it. She said she bought it at a Sarah Coventry party about one year ago. He returned it and left.

Following this incident, she went back into the store. She went to the manager's office and spoke to him about what had happened. He explained that precautions were necessary. She said "I told him I knew that. I was working at Sears at the time... But I didn't understand why they had to go about it the way and in the manner in which they did."

The court dismissed the action for false imprisonment. The evidence showed that the customer was not in fear of the store employees. She freely submitted to the inspection that was requested. Although her conduct shows resentment at the implication that she was a shoplifter, there is no evidence of detention against her will.

13

LORRAINE SABATH COATES v. SCHWEGMANN BROS. GIANT SUPER MARKETS, INC.

COURT OF APPEAL OF LOUISIANA
Fourth Circuit

May 6, 1963

SCHWEGMANN Bros. is a self-service supermarket which requires that customers check packages brought into the store before proceeding to shop. A 3' x 6' sign with 6" lettering and red and green coloring is just inside the store and informs patrons of the requirement to check packages.

Mrs. Coates entered the store carrying a bag containing two children's dresses purchased elsewhere. She cashed her husband's pay check and proceeded to choose two items for purchase still carrying the bag. She proceeded to the cashier's counter and was asked by a store employee what was in the bag. Initially she refused to permit the cashier to inspect the bag.

The cashier said that a search was required and a "floorlady" was summoned. Mrs. Coates allowed the "floorlady" to inspect the contents of the bag. After the inspection the employee stated "it's not our merchandise" and "she can go."

Mrs. Coates brought an action for unlawful search and detention. Mrs. Coates testified that she had been shopping in the store for two years but had no knowledge of the sign warning patrons to check their packages. She also admitted that both the cashier and the "floorlady" were polite, not hostile, and made no threats. A friend of Mrs. Coates who witnessed the incident testified that no one required Mrs. Coates to remain at the counter and she was free to leave when she chose.

The court felt this testimony buttressed the store's testimony that instructions had been issued to store employees to the effect that cashiers were not to detain persons who refuse to permit inspection of packages brought from outside the store, to let them proceed through the line.

The court decided that a serve-yourself store that requires checking of packages purchased elsewhere does so for an obvious reason. The request is a reasonable one. Any humiliation or inconvenience suffered by Mrs. Coates may be attributed directly to her failure to comply with this request. There are three important points brought out by the court in dismissing the action against the store. First, that the customer failed to comply with the request to check the packages. Secondly, that she was not forcibly detained. And finally, that she consented to the inspection of the package.

E. MARIE DELP v.
ZAPP'S DRUG & VARIETY STORES

SUPREME COURT OF OREGON

July 1, 1964

A STATUTE in Oregon at this time allowed a store keeper who had reasonable cause to believe that a customer had committed shoplifting to detain and question the customer for a reasonable time.

Mrs. Delp brought an action for false imprisonment against Zapp's which is a self-service store. She testified that she entered the store carrying a large turkey and a half gallon of milk. She had purchased these items previously at a local grocery store. Mrs. Delp said that she picked up a package of "Rit" which is a small box of dye. She recalled carrying the package in her hand for a while and then placing it in the pocket of her jacket.

Mrs. Delp selected some other items and placed them in the bag containing her groceries. She went to the checkout counter and paid for all the items in the bag but she did not pay for the "Rit."

A store detective stopped her after she had left the checkout area but before she left the store. The detective asked her to come to the back of the store, and Mrs. Delp asked why this was necessary. The store detective replied that she would be told when she got there.

When they arrived in a room in the back of the store, the detective asked Mrs. Delp if she had something in her pocket that she had not paid for. Mrs. Delp said "I felt around and looked around and spied this package of Rit in my pocket, and I felt down and took it out, and said, 'Well, I didn't mean to steal anything like this or take this.' I said, 'I will pay for it.' "

The store detective testified as to the events substantially the same as Mrs. Delp's testimony. The only difference in the

16

testimony was on the question of concealment of the item. Mrs. Delp said the package protruded about a half an inch from the pocket. The detective stated the package was not visible. Mrs. Delp was detained for about thirty minutes. She was asked her name and she continually refused to give this information. The store detective called the police during this time.

She was released and left the store prior to the arrival of the police. As a result two store employees followed her on the street. The police arrived, the store detective restated the facts and they proceeded to stop Mrs. Delp and question her. They checked the items in the bag against the sales slip. The police detained Mrs. Delp for twenty or thirty minutes to check on her record. She was released after this check, and the store refused to press charges.

The first problem before the court was whether the store had reasonable cause to detain Mrs. Delp in the first place. Her allegation was that since the package was partially visible it was not reasonable to suspect her of shoplifting. The court dismissed this argument on the basis that the store cannot be penalized because a potential thief does not satisfactorily conceal the goods. The court found reasonable cause from the events described.

The second issue before the court was whether the duration of the detention was unreasonable. The interrogation was thirty minutes long. The court found the length of time was not unreasonable under the circumstances. The fact that the customer refused to give her name, a basic question in any investigation, helped to prolong the investigation. It warranted calling the police and delaying until they could arrive.

The third allegation by Mrs. Delp was that she was wrongfully detained by the police and the store was liable for the detention.

The court reasoned that regardless of whether the police wrongfully detained Mrs. Delp, the store was not liable based on the facts. Where an officer detains or arrests at the direction of a citizen, that citizen may be liable. Who makes the arrest is not important if the officer acts entirely at the direction of the citizen. But if the citizen merely relates the facts to the officer, who then acts on his own judgment and discretion, then the officer and not the citizen has made the arrest.

Here the officer acted after the facts were related to him. The detention was a result of his own discretion and not directed by the store employees.

WYNONAH DOYLE v.
GLENN DOUGLAS AND STEVE A. DOUGLAS

SUPREME COURT OF OKLAHOMA

March 24, 1964

An action for assault and false imprisonment against a store owner and his agent. The question facing the court was whether or not the store owner had reasonable cause to suspect the customer.

Mrs. Doyle entered the Douglas Big Country Store on January 5, 1961 and purchased $3.60 worth of merchandise. She paid for the items and left the store.

Mrs. Doyle testified that on the front porch of the store she was stopped by Steve A. Douglas. He grabbed her by the arm and accused her of stealing two pounds of bacon and three articles of drugs. She said that she denied this and demanded to be released. Instead, according to Mrs. Doyle, she was forced to submit to a search of her shopping bag, purse, and the lining of her coat.

Mr. Douglas testified that he did not touch Mrs. Doyle and that she voluntarily opened her purse and bag of groceries to disclose their contents. He also denied that he had publicly accused her of theft.

These were the only witnesses who testified as to the events. The jury decides as to the facts after listening to the conflicting testimony. In this case, on the charge of assault, the jury found for the storeowner.

On the issue of false imprisonment, Mr. Douglas testified that prior to January 5, he had on two occasions suspected Mrs. Doyle. This testimony is worth quoting.

Q. "I'll ask you if prior to January 5, 1961, when this incident occurred, had you ever had occasion to observe Mrs.

Doyle?"

A. "Yes, sir."

Q. "I'll ask you whether or not there was anything about the manner in which she shopped that directed your attention to her?"

A. "I had watched a couple of times because certain people, when they come in they have a funny action and if you ever watched people before, why you understand somebody that looks like they are a little suspicious, and I had watched her a couple of times before, prior to that last occasion."

Q. "Mr. Hill, I'll ask you this, had you ever prior to the fifth day of January, 1961, seen Mrs. Doyle take any articles?"

A. "Yes, sir."

Q. "That is, that you felt she was not paying for?"

A. "Yes, sir."

Q. "Now, on these two occasions in question, could you identify the exact item she picked up."

A. "No, sir, I could not, they were small articles and with the distance it would be hard to read that far, but you could tell that she had an article in her hand when she reached for it."

Q. "As I understand you, you could check the total number of items you had seen her take against the total number she paid for?"

A. "That's right."

In this state the legislature had passed a law requiring a store employee to have probable cause before detaining a customer for unlawfully taking merchandise. The testimony of the store owner on a prior act of shoplifting had nothing to do with the incident of January 5, and usually is not admissable. But in this instance, the prior incident is evidence of the store owner's reason for suspecting the customer. In other words the issue of whether he had probable cause to detain Mrs. Doyle is affected by her prior actions and his observations.

The court found that the store owner's detention was for a reasonable cause and extended for a reasonable length of time.

KATHRYN EWING v.
DOSS M. KUTCH AND THE
TRAVELERS INDEMNITY COMPANY

SUPREME COURT OF OKLAHOMA

September 30, 1958

THIS case involves an action by a shopper against a police officer for unlawful arrest.

The police officer, Doss Kutch, testified that he entered Mr. Toma's grocery store about 7 P.M. to do some shopping. He was leaving the store when Mr. Toma told him that Mrs. Ewing had cashed a check to pay for groceries without identifying herself. The check was for $30.00, and there is a state law in Oklahoma making the cashing of a $30.00 bogus check a felony.

Mr. Toma asked Kutch to investigate and pointed out Mrs. Ewing walking away at a fast pace. Kutch followed the shopper to a drugstore where she was cashing a $30.00 check. He told her he had been asked to investigate, but she refused to identify herself and denied she had been in Toma's store. She also refused to go there with him.

The officer then arrested Mrs. Ewing and they returned to Toma's where he discovered that Toma's had not accepted her check and therefore no check had been cashed. They then went to the Sheriff's office. Kutch called the bank and found that the check was good.

A statute in Oklahoma allows a peace officer to arrest a person without a warrant for commission of a felony when reasonable cause exists.

The appeals court judges disagreed as to whether probable or reasonable cause existed in this case. The majority decided that

21

the officer in this case had little or no justification for arresting the shopper. Further, that when he reached Toma's and discovered that no check was cashed, there was no justification whatever for detaining Mrs. Ewing. No one had accused her of committing a felony, he was merely asked to investigate her. Simply to attempt to cash a check without identification is not sufficient reasonable cause to suspect a felony is being attempted.

A minority of judges disagreed with this decision. They stressed the fact that the officer was told that the shopper did cash a check of $30.00. That he saw her walking away at a rapid pace. Also, it was dark, a time when bad check passers tend to operate.

In addition, the dissenting judges cited the shopper's refusal to identify herself or cooperate with the police officer, giving him cause to suspect her motives.

MRS. MARILYN FRUGHT v.
SCHWEGMANN BROS.
GIANT SUPERMARKETS, INC.

COURT OF APPEAL OF LOUISIANA

February 3, 1964

THIS case was a successful action for damages for unlawful detention by the supermarket and the accusation that Mrs. Frught was a shoplifter.

At this time the State of Louisiana had two laws which applied to detention of a shoplifter. The first law in brief allows a peace officer or store employee to use reasonable force to detain a person for a length of time, not to exceed sixty minutes, on the premises, whom he has reasonable ground to believe has committed theft of goods. Said detention shall not constitute an arrest. The second statute frees the officer or employee from writ or criminal liability if he had reasonable grounds for believing at the time of the detention that the person had committed a theft.

The facts of this case are as follows: Mrs. Frught entered the store and selected several small items of a total value of $23.00 for purchase. She checked out with the cashier and paid for these items. She then noticed a sale on small stepladders. She picked up a stepladder, placed it over her grocery cart, returned to the cashier and paid for it.

Mrs. Frught testified she then took the cart to her car in the parking lot and loaded her purchases in the car. She then got into the car and started the motor. At this point she testified that the store detective grabbed her by the arm and took the keys out of the ignition switch. He accused her of shoplifting and demanded she return to the store. She told the detective that there had been some misunderstanding and that she wanted to call her husband.

The store detective testified that he had observed Mrs. Frught shopping and she had taken a buffer pad used for floor waxing, total cost $2.09, and placed it in her purse. He said that he watched her closely from then on and she did not pay for the pad.

He testified that he did not grab Mrs. Frught by the arm, that she returned to the store voluntarily. The remainder of the facts are not disputed. He returned to the store, and questioned the cashier who told him that Mrs. Frught had not paid for the buffer pad.

He then took Mrs. Frught to a storage room that contained no chairs and was about 5' x 9' in area. There were no windows in the room. Another detective joined them, and Mrs. Frught was presented with a form entitled "Confession Blank." The forms were printed in blocks of fifty or one hundred and had been prepared by the store's attorneys.

She refused to sign the confession and asked permission to telephone her husband or the police. The detectives refused her request and also refused to make the telephone calls themselves.

The only alternative presented to her was either to sign the confession or remain in the room. After being held for over thirty minutes she agreed to sign the confession after writing on the bottom "This artical (sic) was taken by me with me thinking I had paid for it." The detectives agreed to the addition.

Mrs. Frught testified that she signed the confession only after her repeated requests to call her husband were refused. She and her husband operated a day nursery and she was due to drive the children home. After leaving the store she drove home, became very upset and hysterical. Her husband gave her nerve medicine and put her to bed. He called the police and they returned to the store where the store employees refused to return the confession.

The question before the court was whether the store employee had reasonable grounds for detaining Mrs. Frught so as to be relieved of liability under the statute.

The court found against the store and its employee and awarded Mrs. Frught $1,500.00 in damages. In coming to this conclusion the judge pointed out several failings on the part of the store detective.

At no time had the detective checked the purchases against the sales slip although he had the opportunity to do so from the outset. His sole purpose in detaining Mrs. Frught was to obtain a confession, and not to properly investigate in order to make a determination as to the facts. Mrs. Frught did not have a choice in returning to the store, and she was held against her will.

Although he testified that he had watched her closely while she was in the store, he admitted that he did not see her select the stepladder and go back to pay for it. He was not close enough to the cashier to hear the conversation which took place there.

In actual fact, Mrs. Frught was a regular customer, knew the cashier, and told her the price of the buffer pad and paid for it. The cashier violated a store rule in ringing up an item not visible to her, but the detective assumed Mrs. Frught guilty rather than that the cashier had violated the store regulation.

Further, one of the detectives who aided in intimidating Mrs. Frught into a confession had no knowledge whatsoever of the circumstances, since he made no personal observations or investigations.

By relying on the cashier's memory, the detective did not have reasonable grounds to hold Mrs. Frught. He acted unreasonably in not using the sales slip to determine immediately the facts before detaining Mrs. Frught and obtaining a confession.

BETTIE GROOMES v.
UNITED STATES OF AMERICA

MUNICIPAL COURT OF APPEALS FOR
THE DISTRICT OF COLUMBIA

June 29, 1959

THE defendant in the case was convicted of larceny for shoplifting. The defense maintained that the Government failed to establish sufficient proof of a taking and carrying away of the property involved in the theft.

The defendant was shopping in a contained self-service market. Her shopping cart had several grocery items and her purse. A store employee observed her take two items from a shelf, place them in her purse, and put the purse back in the shopping cart.

She then looked about for a moment and continued around the store. During this time she was watched by a clerk and a store manager, who ultimately followed her toward the checkout counter.

The defendant saw the two employees following her, and walked back toward them. She handed over the two articles in her purse.

The store manager testified that he identified the articles as belonging to the store through their markings. One of the items was a package of meat that was still cold. Defendant testified that the items were given to her by a friend earlier in the day.

The defense maintained that this evidence failed to establish that defendant had dominion and complete control over the property. She had not passed the checkout counter. The items were not concealed on her person, but still in the shopping cart which belonged to the store. The defense also pointed out that she was detained by the store manager while still in the store.

26

The court in finding the defendant guilty, pointed out that larceny is a crime involving wrongful possession and taking away of someone's property. When the crime occurs in a self-service store, the burden of proof is heavier on the state's part. This is because this system of merchandising invites the patron to take possession of the goods. Possession does not pass title, and is conditional until purchase is made at the check-out counter.

The evidence in this case showed defendant's actions were entirely inconsistent with a prospective purchase. The items were immediately secreted in a purse. Although the purse was in the shopping cart, the items were separated from the other items in the cart. Defendant was exercising complete control over these items.

The element of taking away another's property is satisfied by showing the articles were concealed and ready for convenient removal. Whether or not they were ever actually removed is immaterial.

Finally, the court dealt with the question of whether defendant had the necessary intent to steal. This is question for the jury, to be determined by all the evidence. The fact that defendant returned the merchandise voluntarily does not alter the original taking.

MARIE HALES v.
McCRORY-McLELLAN CORPORATION

SUPREME COURT OF NORTH CAROLINA

November 27, 1963

Miss Hales sued the McCrory-McLellan Corporation for false imprisonment. The store is a self-service type, merchandise on shelves for selection by customers and payment at checkout.

On September 3, 1960 Miss Hales went to the store to return certain articles she had bought there previously. She said she wanted different sizes of the same merchandise. She was carrying the items in a bag.

The store manager came over to her at the checkout counter and said "Come over here with me. You know what for." He ordered another employee to call the police. Miss Hales and the store manager waited for the police at the end of the counter.

The police arrived and they entered a little room. The store manager told the policeman that he saw Miss Hales come down with a bag and he knew what the bag was for. He agreed to "sign papers" when asked to do so by the police officer.

Another store employee entered the room at this point and said he knew what it was about and to go ahead and sign papers.

The police officer then escorted Miss Hales to the police department. There she gave her name and address and answered other questions before being released.

The question presented on this sequence of events is whether the restraint was unlawful. The court found first that Miss Hales was innocent of any shoplifting charge. It reviewed the circumstances, and mentioned the fact that two different employees accused Miss Hales of theft. And further, two

28

policemen were present and papers were to be signed.

Under the circumstances the court felt Miss Hales could reasonably believe that she was under restraint from the actions and words of the store employees.

It is important to note that the employees of the store made no attempt whatsoever to investigate the facts. This omission probably strongly influenced the court in coming to its decision.

HENRY JACOBSMA v.
GOLDBERG'S FASHION FORUM

APPELLATE COURT OF ILLINOIS
FIRST DISTRICT, FIRST DIVISION

September 24, 1973

THE customer in this case is bringing a personal injury action against the store for injuries sustained by him when he attempted to stop a fleeing shoplifter.

On January 15, 1966 Mr. and Mrs. Jacobsma entered Goldberg's, which is located in the Ford City shopping center. There were very few customers in the store at the time. Mr. Jacobsma was inside the store for about twenty feet, when he observed the store manager about seventy-five feet down an aisle and another man running down the same aisle towards him. There were no other men in the store.

The manager shouted "Stop thief" and appeared to be pointing in the direction of Mr. Jacobsma. Mr. Jacobsma then grabbed the suspected shoplifter and they both fell to the floor. Some clothes fell from under the man's coat and he got up and ran out.

Mr. Jacobsma was unable to get up without assistance, and he was taken to a hospital where his injury was diagnosed as a dislocated shoulder.

Ordinarily the status of a customer in a store is that of a business invitee, and the store owes a duty of exercising ordinary care in regard to his safety. An issue presented at this trial was whether the customer had lost his status as a business invitee and become a volunteer, which requires a lesser duty on the store's part.

The key to the customer's status was whether or not the store manager's actions could be construed as a request for assistance. The court felt it was a cry for help and therefore the customer here was not a volunteer.

Since the customer's status was that of a business invitee the duty owed him by the store was that of ordinary care. In order for Mr. Jacobsma to recover then, some negligence on the store's part must be shown.

Ordinarily there is no liability on the store's part for injuries caused by a third person's criminal acts where the store had no knowledge of previous problems or circumstances so that danger could be anticipated.

In this case, however, evidence brought out at the trial indicated the same shoplifter who caused the injury had been in the store three days before and had attempted to steal some clothing. Therefore the store manager had knowledge of a prior crime. The jury could find that he was charged with the responsibility of protecting his customers and failed to do so in this situation.

The court discussed the fact that the store had no security patrol or devices such as alarm systems as protection. The court upheld the jury verdict against the store for negligent failure to protect its customer.

JACQUELINE MAINES JANNEY v. ARLAN'S DEPARTMENT STORE

U. S. DISTRICT COURT
W. D. Virginia

November 15, 1965

MRS. Janney brought an action against Arlan's for malicious prosecution based on the theory that a store employee caused her arrest without justification.

On December 12, 1964 while shopping in Arlan's, Mrs. Janney picked up several articles of merchandise. The testimony was in conflict on whether she concealed the merchandise in her handbag or carried it under her arm.

She was asked to go to a room in the store by an employee. There she was questioned and signed a confession. After signing the confession, Mrs. Janney was escorted from the store.

Mrs. Janney was arrested and tried for concealing merchandise. She was convicted and later acquitted on appeal.

The original arrest warrant was issued by a police detective who was also an employee of the department store.

The court dismissed the action. It reasoned that even if the store, through its employee, had caused the arrest warrant to be issued, the store had probable cause to believe the customer was concealing goods.

KNIGHT v.
POWERS DRY GOODS CO., INC.

SUPREME COURT OF MINNESOTA

January 9, 1948

THIS is an action by a customer against the store for injuries received when an escaping shoplifter knocked the customer down. The theory of the case is that the store failed to use reasonable care in protecting the customer and should have known of the danger presented by the shoplifter.

On February 2, 1945 a bookstore owner saw a man standing on a corner that he thought to be a book thief. The man, later identified as Vancil Ingall, was carrying a box 18″ to 24″ long and 10″ high.

The next day Ingall entered the bookstore. The owner told his assistant to watch him. The assistant "made herself obnoxious to him, asking if she could help him." Finally he left and the owner of the store called all the other bookstores in town to be alert, supplying a description of Ingall.

The store owner had met Ingall before and testified that Ingall was well dressed, acted the part of a perfect gentleman. He seemed to be educated, and did not act like a thief or criminal. He said that Ingall was not the type of man to threaten or fight.

A short time later Ingall entered Powers Dry Goods Store. Two women detectives employed by the store had received the warning, and went to the book department. They had no information other than the fact that there was a book thief in town.

One detective went outside and watched Ingall through the window, the other observed him from inside. Ingall proceeded to stack some books on the floor and then shove them inside the trick box. One detective described Ingall as looking "more like a retired minister than anything else."

Ingall left the store and was stopped on the sidewalk by the detective. He said "Pardon me, sir, but don't you think you had better pay for those books?" Ingall replied in a soft, gentle voice, "I guess I will." He then turned around and calmly walked ahead of the detective into the store, making no attempt to escape.

On the way to the book department the store detective took hold of his arm and said "There are too many people here. Let's go to the office, it will be less conspicuous. They then proceeded together, walking quietly to the elevator. While standing in front of the elevator, Ingall suddenly threw the box and ran. This was his first showing of any violent propensities.

The detective testified that as Ingall was running down the aisle, Mrs. Knight, a customer, took several steps toward him. Mrs. Knight was sixty-seven years old at the time, and was carrying a cane. Ingall knocked her down as she was the only person between him and escape.

Mrs. Knight was first taken to the coffee shop. She said she was glad she had tried to stop him; that she felt she had done her duty as a citizen. She seemed very elated. She was taken to the nurse's office on the fourth floor. She said that "there should be a big reward out for him, and she should be the one to get the reward, she would be entitled to it because she had stopped him."

Mrs. Knight testified rather differently. She said "Just then I heard an awful noise, kind of moaning, of a lot of women groaning and crying, so I went across the aisle there. . . . So I was standing there and trying to find out about it, and all of a sudden this wild looking being, with his hair all disheveled, his necktie untied, was leaping on the ground this way, then he went over crossways, stood there, looked me right in the eye, and without a moment's notice he came right towards me, and I never budged from where I was standing. I never budged from that spot. As he came toward me, I was just terror stricken, I was so frightened I didn't know who he was. His hair was all up, he looked like Charles Laughton of the movies. He was a fellow twice my size, almost three hundred pounds, huge, far too big for any police to tackle. They refused to do it. And he was standing over there and he looked me right in the eye. And he had plenty of time to get out because there was a broad aisle. And there wasn't a soul there except myself. And he came toward me. Without a moment's warning he grabbed me right across my wrist, fractured my arm. He kicked my leg so when I went to get up I was on the floor.... These two detectives weren't anywhere near the place ... and the stick went away to the ceiling, came down, sounded with a report that was just deafening.... When he got up to me, he got almost past me, all of a sudden he turned around, grabbed my wrist, twisted it around, and the stick went high up, just like an explosion, came down to the floor, and he kicked my leg right out of the socket. I went down on the floor, and became semiconscious."

She denied making any statement about a citizen's duty, although she admitted that there was "some kidding" about rewards. She said she had to wait a half an hour for the nurse.

Mrs. Knight's doctor testified that she told him she noticed several people chasing a thief. She attempted to stop him with a ski pole. She said she either tried to trip him or strike him with it.

The question presented was whether the store must use reasonable care to protect its customers from vicious persons brought into the store whether or not the store employees knew the person to be vicious. The court flatly stated that this is not a proper test of the store's obligation. The store is not responsible for a person's conduct when it has no prior knowledge of any violent conduct on his part. Therefore, the proper test is whether the store had such knowledge prior to the act, and acted negligently in not taking proper precautions against possible harm to the customers.

In this case Mrs. Knight did not offer any evidence whatsoever that would lead one to believe Ingall was vicious. All the evidence supported the belief that Ingall was quiet, distinguished looking, and rather docile. When asked to pay for the books in front of the store, he quietly walked to the elevator.

Knowledge that Ingall was a shoplifter is not the same thing as knowledge that he was vicious.

Therefore, the store employees were not negligent in walking Ingall to the elevator because they had no reason to know that he was capable of violence.

JESSIE E. LUKAS v.
J. C. PENNEY COMPANY

SUPREME COURT OF OREGON

February 14, 1963

THE customer in this case is bringing an action against J. C. Penney for false imprisonment, alleging she was wrongfully detained upon a false claim of shoplifting a dress.

A statute in this state allows a merchant to detain a person for a reasonable time when the merchant has reasonable cause for believing that such person has committed the crime of shoplifting.

On November 11, 1959 Mrs. Lukas and her granddaughter entered J. C. Penney's. They went to the second floor dress department looking for a dress for the granddaughter, named Barbara. Barbara was carrying a shopping bag containing some work clothes belonging to her.

Mrs. Lukas and Barbara chose two dresses from a rack and tried them on, there being no clerk present. A clerk did arrive and chose a few more dresses for them. The two found one white dress they considered buying, but decided to try another store before making a purchase. At this time the clerk was gone and Mrs. Lukas testified she returned the dresses to the racks. They were hurrying for fear the other store would close since it was getting late. Mrs. Lukas testified that they were out of the store and on the street when a man ran up and said they had a white dress in the shopping bag. Barbara asked him for credentials before allowing him to look in the bag. He said he didn't need any and started pulling at the bag. All three held onto the bag for a time, and a crowd gathered.

Mrs. Lukas said she became frightened, Barbara began to cry, so

36

she gave up the bag. The store employee looked into it, found no dress, and then returned to the store.

The store clerk agreed that she was waiting on a customer when Jessie Lukas and Barbara entered the dress department. She waited on them, and they chose the white dress. She then waited on another customer and when she returned to finalize the sale, they were gone. She checked the rack and did not find the white dress. The clerk reported the incident, and after a thorough search, the white dress could not be found.

The store employee who went after Mrs. Lukas, a Mr. Hale, admitted that he didn't identify himself when he accosted Mrs. Lukas and Barbara in the street. He did not show any credentials. He did use physical force to obtain possession of the bag.

The court found that the clerk's testimony warranted a reasonable belief in the store employee that shoplifting had occurred. The fact that the dress was not found and the presence of the shopping bag, etc. The court explained that probable cause is usually a close question but an attempt must be made to balance the rights of the merchant in his goods with the rights of liberty of the customer.

The court agreed that Mr. Hales had acted unreasonably by not identifying himself or asking Mrs. Lukas to return to the store. The jury in this case believed the testimony of Mrs. Lukas, that the dress had been returned, and found no probable cause to detain her.

PAMELA SUE PEAK v.
W. T. GRANT COMPANY

KANSAS CITY COURT OF APPEALS
MISSOURI

December 7, 1964

ON December 15, 1962 Pamela, age sixteen, entered the W. T. Grant store with her mother; younger sister, age thirteen; and brother, age twelve. The purpose of the trip was to do their Christmas shopping. The children had $5.00 each to spend, and separated on entering the store so that no one would know what the other purchased. Pamela's mother went to a drugstore by herself.

Mrs. Howard, an employee of the store, saw Pamela's sister, Candy, trying to close her purse. She said it was so full it was difficult to close. She testified "I didn't see her put anything in her purse." When she approached Candy, her face got red and she hurried to another end of the store.

This incident was reported to a Mr. Knapp, who was watching for shoplifters. Mr. Knapp and a security officer followed Candy for three or four minutes. Candy's actions seemed to be evasive as she went around several counters. She met her brother and they went beyond the checkstand to the door.

The security officer stopped Candy, identified himself, and told her she was suspected of shoplifting. Candy did not give up the purse on request. Her brother told her to show the purse but she refused.

Candy's brother left and returned with Pamela. When she arrived and was told what had happened, she asked to see a uniformed police officer. Mr. Knapp asked that they all go to the basement where the store offices were located.

Pamela testified that at this point Knapp took hold of Candy's arm. She then tried to leave, taking Candy by the arm. The security officer grabbed her by the coat. Pamela said she would scream if he didn't let go; he started to shake her and she screamed. She testified that the officer threw her into a rack of clothes and she struck her back. A fight ensued, Pamela kicking the officer and striking him with a package.

A witness testified that Pamela continued to scream and Knapp covered her mouth with his hand and dragged her toward the back of the store. She struck against several counters on the way down the aisle.

A crowd of about forty people had gathered to watch. Pamela's mother, the store manager, and a police officer now arrived on the scene. Pam's mother took the purse and handed it to the security officer. It contained nothing belonging to the store. The Peak family then left the store.

Knapp and the security officer testified that the purse was much thinner than it had been at the time they first saw it. Knapp also testified that he had not seen Candy a short time before her mother arrived, yet he did not see her leave the group.

The court denied the defense of a statue allowing detention of a suspected shoplifter for reasonable cause, since Pamela was never suspected of any crime. She was wrongfully detained because it was her sister who was the suspect.

The store defended itself on the theory that Knapp had exceeded his authority, had left the scope of his employment. Therefore, the store argued, he was not an agent at the time and the responsibility of his acts cannot be transferred to his employer.

The store admitted that part of Knapp's duties was to watch for and apprehend shoplifters. However, it argued that he violated his written instructions quoted as follows: "Never detain a person on uncorroborated word of a saleswoman or customer as they may be mistaken. Before anyone is detained and brought back to the store be sure that there is not any doubt of guilt, for once arrest is made, withdrawal of charge cannot save company from liability. Never cause an arrest unless evidence is so strong that conviction is inevitable. It is better that a guilty shoplifter be allowed to escape justice occasionally rather than subject company to suits for false arrest."

Whether or not the store as principal is liable for the acts of its agent depends on whether the acts were authorized or ratified by the store. In this case Knapp was definitely authorized to arrest shoplifters. Even though he may have violated the written instructions of the store, he is still working within the scope of his employment. He is furthering the objective he was hired for, to arrest shoplifters. Therefore the store is also liable for his conduct.

J. C. PENNEY COMPANY, INC. v.
MRS. DELLA COX

SUPREME COURT OF MISSISSIPPI

January 14, 1963

IN this case Mrs. Cox was successful in her action of false imprisonment against the store.

On April 1, 1961 at about 2 P.M. Mrs. Cox entered J. C. Penney Co. to do some shopping. She was carrying a paper bag containing a pair of shoes. She stopped in the front of the store at a counter containing cosmetics and lipsticks. The counter was within the building on a platform about three steps up from the floor.

The assistant manager came up to Mrs. Cox, caught her by the arm, and demanded that she pay him for the deodorant that she had in the paper bag and in her purse. He demanded she open the bag and purse and place the contents on the steps which she did.

This took place in view of all the salespeople and customers at the front of the store. Mrs. Cox testified that "I was never so humiliated in my life. I had never stolen anything and I just wanted to cry and just went all to pieces. It really made me sick."

The manager admitted his mistake as soon as he saw that she did not have what he was looking for. None of the store employees testified that they saw Mrs. Cox take anything. One saleslady said that Mrs. Cox acted suspicious and that another customer told her "I think she put something in her bag." This information was passed on to another clerk who told the manager about it.

The store's defense to the action consisted of the fact that it was justified in making the inquiries. The court had to decide whether the store acted in good faith, on a reasonable belief that its actions were justified. More than mere conjecture or suspicion is necessary. A store cannot subject its customers to humiliation and disgrace on the mere whim of management.

The court found the store had exceeded its authority in the situation. No one saw Mrs. Cox take anything. In addition, the method of investigation was unreasonable. Grabbing the customer in full view of others, and demanding she display her possessions amounted to embarrassing and harassing Mrs. Cox.

J. C. PENNEY COMPANY v.
OPAL O'DANIELL

UNITED STATES COURT OF APPEALS

January 29, 1959

ON December 9, 1957 Opal O'Daniell went to Penney's in Oklahoma City to make some purchases. Another customer shopping in the store at the same time saw someone take two gowns from a display table and lower them to a sack. The customer testified she heard the rustling of a paper sack. She saw the woman hurriedly leave the main floor after observing that she was being watched. She was carrying a large paper bag.

A description of the customer and the incident was given to the manager. A customer meeting the description given was located on the second floor by an employee.

The store manager approached her and she went to the elevator to the main floor. She left the store and was followed by the store manager and another employee. The woman with the sack was followed through several stores and finally onto a bus. The store manager also boarded the bus. She changed seats on the bus three times and finally at the rear of the bus began fooling with the bag.

Finally, the bus was stopped by the police. The sack was examined and a nightgown with a Penney's label was found. She explained its presence by saying that she received it as a present a year before and wanted to exchange it. The woman with the sack was Opal O'Daniell. She was returned at her request to the store where it was determined that the nightgown in the sack was not on display at the store.

Mrs. O'Daniell sued the store for false imprisonment based on the above-stated facts. However, the court did not allow the case to go to the jury. The test to be met by the store is whether probable

43

cause existed for their actions. In other words, would reasonably minded persons under the circumstances conclude that cause of detention existed?

The court found that the store employees in this case acted reasonably. All the evidence including Mrs. O'Daniell's suspicious actions, pointed to the fact that she had taken some property. The fact that she did not is not enough to warrant a finding of false imprisonment.

GEORGINA PRIETO v. THE MAY DEPARTMENT STORES COMPANY

DISTRICT OF COLUMBIA COURT OF APPEALS

November 22, 1965

AN action against the department store for false arrest, false imprisonment and malicious prosecution.

Georgina Prieto entered the store's basement department just prior to closing time. She examined a pair of pajamas at the counter. A saleswoman offered her assistance, and the customer expressed her interest in trying on the garments.

At that time the closing bell rang and the saleswoman informed the customer of the store closing. The customer stated "Don't worry about me because I don't buy nothing." The saleslady closed the register and left.

A store detective then observed the customer place the pajamas over her left arm and proceed to the escalator. She arrived at the main floor and walked towards a door opening on the street. The store detective stopped her before she left the store and informed her that she had not paid for the pajamas. She replied that she had forgotten them, that she didn't want them. The detective escorted her to the office where she was questioned and the police were notified.

Only two facts were in dispute at the trial. The detective testified that the price tag was removed by the customer in the basement, and that when he stopped her they were in the vestibule, through the first set of doors. She denied removal of the price tag and said she was stopped before she reached the vestibule.

The circumstances of this case are similar to the Rothstein case, and the question to be decided by the court is the same. Did the

45

store employee have probable cause to initiate the course of action taken? Would a reasonably prudent police officer or store detective in observing the customer's actions, reasonably believe that she was in the act of committing a theft?

The court decided that the facts would give a store employee reasonable grounds to suspect a theft and dismissed the action. In making the decision the court stressed that the store was not obligated to prove an actual attempted theft or what was the customer's intent. Whether or not she had forgotten the pajamas, or overlooked them, or might have returned them on discovery is not an issue. The store detective's actions are to be judged by what he observed and not the customer's state of mind.

ALMA RADLOFF ET AL v.
NATIONAL FOOD STORES, INC.

SUPREME COURT OF WISCONSIN

June 4, 1963

THIS was an action against a storekeeper for injuries sustained when a shoplifter, who was attempting to escape from store employees, ran into a customer.

The facts in the case were as follows:

On the afternoon on January 9, 1961 at approximately 1:30 P.M., Alma Radloff and her husband, Carl Radloff, were shopping in a National Foods store located in Milwaukee, Wisconsin.

During the time that the Radloffs were doing their shopping, an employee of the store, named Robert Young, noticed that a man had picked up two cartons of cigarettes from the cigarette counter and placed them under his jacket. Mr. Young and another employee, Mr. Erickson, followed the suspected shoplifter through the store and saw that at the checkout counter he only paid for a loaf of bread, never revealing that he had the cigarettes under his coat.

Erickson and Young then followed the shoplifter outside and confronted him either in the vestibule of the store, as Young testified, or immediately outside the store, as Erickson testified. The employees then asked the shoplifter if he would please come back into the store and he replied "No, you're going to gang up on me." The employees assured him that they were not going to gang up on him and again asked him to please come back into the store, to which he agreed. The two employees and the shoplifter then reentered the store.

The three men walked down one of the aisles of the

supermarket towards the rear of the store, with Young in front of the shoplifter and Erickson behind him. When they were about one fourth of the way down the aisle, the cigarettes suddenly fell out from under the shoplifter's coat and onto the floor. As Erickson bent down to pick up the cigarettes, the shoplifter quickly turned around, pushed Erickson to the floor and ran out the front exit of the store. As the shoplifter ran through the checkout aisle, Erickson yelled at him to stop. The shoplifter did not heed the warning but ran into Mrs. Radloff, knocking her down and causing the injuries which furnish the basis of this law suit.

There was some dispute as to the size of the alleged shoplifter but there was testimony that he was around 5 feet, 11 inches tall, and weighed 190 to 200 pounds. From the time that Erickson was knocked down by the shoplifter until Mrs. Radloff was thrown to the floor, only a few seconds elapsed. All parties agreed that the only possible egress from the store was through one of the four checkout aisles located at the front of the store, and that at the time that the incident took place, two of the checkout counters were closed to customer traffic.

The jury awarded $6,178.35 to the Radloffs and the defendant storekeeper filed an appeal to the Supreme Court of Wisconsin.

The basic issue presented to the court was, What duty does a storekeeper owe to a customer to protect that customer from injuries caused to him by the intentional acts of an escaping shoplifter?

Before deciding this issue, however, the court discussed the legal rule in Wisconsin governing the authority of storekeepers in dealing with shoplifters detected in the act of shoplifting on their premises.

Quoting from a previous decision, the Court stated, "An arrest without a warrant has never been lawful except in those cases where the public security requires it; and this has only been recognized in a felony, and in breaches of the peace committed in the presence of an officer."

Thus, when Young spotted the shoplifter putting the cigarettes under his coat, it would have been unlawful, at that time, for him to make an arrest. This is especially true when we consider the fact that the alleged shoplifter could well have paid for the items at the time that he went to the checkout counter.

The defendant's employees were not negligent, *per se*, in stopping the shoplifter to recover the goods he had stolen for certainly these employees had the right to recover their employer's goods. But they had no right to arrest the shoplifter, as the alleged crime was a misdemeanor and the employees of the National Food Store did not have a warrant to arrest the shoplifter.

Furthermore, it is quite obvious that under existing and well-established legal rules, the supermarket employees had to be extremely careful in apprehending a customer suspected of shoplifting, because if subsequent events showed that the person suspected had not in fact been shoplifting, then a suit for false imprisonment would be inevitable. For these reasons, Erickson and Young asked the shoplifter to return to the store voluntarily, and the testimony established that the shoplifter consented to return without compulsion.

In reversing the judgment of the lower court, the Wisconsin Supreme Court determined that none of the evidence established that the proprietor knew or by the exercise of reasonable care, could have discovered that the shoplifter was going to attempt to break loose and rush out of the store, bumping into customers that might be in the way.

The Court stated that the Radloffs' case rested on three facts in the record with respect to the shoplifter:

1. That he was a Negro, rugged looking, around 5 feet, 11 inches, and weighed 190 to 200 pounds.
2. That the shoplifter, when initially returning to the store, tried to keep a counter between Young and Erickson; and
3. That originally, when the shoplifter was apprehended, he stated to Young and Erickson, after he was requested to return to the store, "You people are going to gang up on me."

The Court then stated: "In our opinion, none of this evidence, taken either individually or cumulatively, was sufficient to raise a jury question. We, therefore, conclude that as a matter of law, the defendant did not know and by the exercise of reasonable care could not have discovered that the violent acts done by the shoplifter were being done or were about to be done so as to give rise to a duty on the part of the defendant to protect its customers from the shoplifter's acts.''

Judgment was reversed and the case remanded to the Circuit Court for the purpose of dismissing the complaint.

JAMES P. ROGERS v.
SEARS, ROEBUCK & COMPANY

SUPREME COURT OF WASHINGTON

May 17, 1956

ON December 5, 1952 Mr. Rogers, accompanied by his eleven-year-old daughter, entered Sears and purchased an electrical outlet. The cost of the merchandise was 57¢. On returning home he discovered that a part of the outlet was missing, namely the faceplate.

On the next day, December 6th, he returned to the store carrying the outlet. He showed it to a clerk, Elmer VanHoose and asked for a faceplate. No faceplate was available in his color. Mr. Rogers then put the outlet in his pocket and left the store. He went to a local store and bought the faceplate.

Meanwhile the Sears clerk, Elmer VanHoose, was following him, apparently believing he had stolen the outlet. When VanHoose left the store he told a clerk to notify Mr. Olson, the security officer.

VanHoose spotted Rogers in an electrical shop and he called the police. As Rogers left this store, VanHoose and the police officer held him by the arm. VanHoose said "That is the man officer." VanHoose accused Rogers of stealing the outlet. He told the police officer that he saw Rogers take it from a counter. All three then proceeded to the police station. At this time it was about 11 A.M. Although the time was disputed, Rogers was held in the police station until about 2 P.M. He was never booked or arrested.

The police officer asked VanHoose if he was sure that Rogers stole the item. VanHoose said, "I seen you do it, don't deny it." VanHoose later called the store and explained his whereabouts.

51

The store manager told him to do nothing, that he was sending Mr. Olson over. He also said to VanHoose "You sure got us into a peck of trouble."

Olson arrived, questioned Rogers who suggested he call his daughter. Olson did this and returned saying, "I think there has been an awful mistake on somebody's part." Rogers was released.

False imprisonment is the unlawful restraint by words or acts of the physical liberty of another. It is clear from the facts that Rogers was unlawfully detained by VanHoose. The contention that he could have walked away because he was not under arrest is without merit. No one just walks away from a police officer.

Having found the clerk guilty of false imprisonment, the court turned to the question of whether the store was responsible for the actions of its clerk. The court found that the clerk was not acting within the scope of his employment when he restrained Rogers. The clerks were instructed at regular meetings as to what they should do if they see an article being stolen. They were never instructed to accuse a customer, but rather to inform the store security employees. The clerk in this instance left the store to restrain Rogers, and was clearly not within the scope of his employment.

The next problem faced by the court was whether Sears had ratified the clerk's actions after it had knowledge. If this were the case, Sears would be liable for his acitons. The court dismissed any possibility here. As soon as VanHoose called the store, the manager sent a security man to the police station. He promptly investigated and released Rogers. Therefore, the store did not ratify the clerk's actions and was free from fault in this instance.

SYLVIA ROTHSTEIN v. JACKSON'S OF CORAL GABLES, INC.

DISTRICT COURT OF APPEAL OF FLORIDA
Third District

October 2, 1961

THIS was an action for both false arrest and false imprisonment. While shopping inside the department store, Sylvia Rothstein placed an article of merchandise around her waist. She then proceeded to move away from the counter where she obtained the merchandise. There were no sales personnel in the area at the time. A store employee took her into custody and recovered the merchandise.

In Florida there is a statute which applies directly to this situation. The statute provides in substance that a merchant's employee, who has probable cause to believe that goods belonging to the merchant have been unlawfully taken, can recover them by taking the person into custody for the purpose of effecting a recovery of the merchandise. However, the detention must be in a reasonable manner and for a reasonable time.

The court determined that the store employee's suspicions could be aroused by the customer's actions, and therefore he could determine whether or not the merchandise had been secreted for the purpose of evading payment. The undisputed facts made no showing that the store employee's actions were unreasonable or without basis in fact.

The question to be determined in judging the employee's conduct is not whether an actual larceny had been committed, but rather whether he had probable cause to believe one was committed. The facts then, showed probable cause as required by the statute and the action against the store was dismissed.

SAFEWAY STORES, INC. v.
KENNETH AMBURN

COURT OF CIVIL APPEALS OF TEXAS

March 12, 1965

KENNETH Amburn was an employee of Safeway Stores, and brought an action for false imprisonment on the facts which follow.

At about 9:30 A.M., Amburn was working at the store when he recognized the District Manager. About an hour later, he was loading produce on a truck when the District Manager tapped him on the shoulder and asked him to go along with him to talk to somebody.

They proceeded to a secluded area in the back of the store, actually an aisle that was twelve feet long and six feet wide. A Mr. Koch who was employed by a security company was waiting there. Koch questioned Amburn for about thirty to forty minutes. No physical force was used to detain Amburn who testified that at all times the aisle was open and he could have used it to leave. No one told him that he had to remain where he was.

Amburn testified that Koch said he had checked the register tapes and had enough evidence to send him to the penitentiary. Amburn said when he saw the tapes he became ill. He said his knees were weak and he doesn't think he could have moved if he wanted to do so.

Koch dictated a letter which Amburn wrote and signed admitting to the theft of $500.00. Later that day Amburn went home, cleaned out his car and returned. He signed over title to the car to Safeway Stores and a note to Safeway for $280.00. Amburn was then discharged.

The court found no evidence of false imprisonment. As an

employer-employee relationship existed, the logical place to discuss the fidelity of the employee was at his place of employment. No threats were made. Amburn could have left at any time.

The court disapproved of Koch's conduct in obtaining the confession and the title to the car. However, these matters did not relate to the charge of false imprisonment.

Amburn's testimony that he was so afraid he could not leave does not amount to being restricted. If a person can leave by ordinary means, he is not being detained.

CASE 24

SAFEWAY STORES v.
HEZZIE C. BARRACK

COURT OF APPEALS OF MARYLAND

May 8, 1956

ON September 3, 1954 the customer entered the Safeway store carrying two bundles of laundry and a large bag in which were other purchases bought at another store. He placed these articles in a pushcart and began shopping. He selected many articles for purchase and placed them in the shopping cart, after which he took the pushcart to the checkout counter. Before going through the checkout, he left the cart to pick up a carton and load his purchases.

After paying for his selections he began loading them from the shopping cart to the carton. Mr. Barrack testified that as he lifted the laundry bag from the shopping cart a pound of butter fell to the floor. He had picked this article out but had not paid for it.

A store employee named Smith who was wearing a badge came up and accused him of trying to steal the butter. Smith also picked up a box of pepper and accused him of stealing that. Barrack testified that he offered to pay but Smith told the checkout girl not to take the money, that he was going to have him locked up.

Barrack said he left the store and went into the street where Smith followed him. Smith called him names and ordered him inside according to Barrack. The police arrived, charged him with stealing, and he was removed to the police station where he was placed in a cell.

The store employee, Smith, told a different story. He said he watched Barrack pick up the butter and put it in a paper bag that he had brought into the store. He also said he saw him place the pepper in his pocket. He said he watched Barrack put both the butter and the pepper in the carton and start to leave.

Smith testified that Barrack got very mean and nasty at the checkout stand. "He got so nasty, I got kind of mean myself." In the backroom Barrack offered to pay double the amount of the merchandise rather than have any trouble.

Smith said that he had instructions from his superior to "use my own discretion if people acted nasty, just do what I wanted to do with them. He told me then he wasn't going to stop at any means of helping to protect the company's property."

Smith further testified that "I hardly ever lock anybody up who is actually halfway decent and sorry they did it or they have some good excuse and they say they are not going to do it again. If I locked everybody up I caught, I would probably be in court all the time."

Barrack was tried and found not guilty of stealing the merchandise. He then brought an action for false imprisonment and for malicious prosecution.

In order to find false imprisonment, there must be a deprivation of liberty without consent or legal cause. The jury in this case had two differing views as to the sequence of events. When this happens the jury is free to decide which is to be believed. In this case the jury found for the customer.

Barrack also was successful in his action for malicious prosecution. There are four necessary elements to prove that there is a case of malicious proseuction.

First, Barrack had to show a criminal proceeding was instituted by Smith. Secondly that he was found not guilty at that proceeding. Next, Barrack must prove that there was no probable cause for the proceeding in the first place, and finally that the proceeding was brought by Smith with malice.

If the primary purpose for bringing the action is one other than bringing an offender to justice, malice is present.

Barrack was able to show all four elements. He was tried for stealing and he was found not guilty. The jury could believe his story that there was no intent to steal and therefore probable cause was lacking.

Finally, malice could be shown from Smith's own testimony. He said that he did not prosecute all offenders, only those who were not properly sorry for their act and who did not admit it. He almost said that he prosecuted because of Barrack's attitude towards him.

ARTHUR J. SENNETT v.
TED ZIMMERMAN

SUPREME COURT OF WASHINGTON

August 1, 1957

ON August 7, 1954 Arthur Sennett was shopping in a Pay Less drugstore operated by Ted Zimmerman. He was watched while shopping by a store detective, Marcelyn Falin.

The store detective was also a deputy city police officer. When Mr. Sennett left the store, he was stopped by the store detective and returned to a back room in the store. He was detained in the room until the police arrived and then was taken into custody. He appealed a conviction for petty larceny and was acquitted at a jury trial. Mr. Sennett then brought an action against the store and the detective for false arrest and false imprisonment.

The issue in this case is the capacity of the store detective. An ordinary citizen cannot make an arrest for a misdemeanor unless he can show that the misdemeanor was actually committed in his presence.

A police officer, on the other hand, may make an arrest without a warrant for a misdemeanor, if he has reasonable cause to believe that it is taking place in his presence. The difference is that in one case the crime must have actually taken place while in the other it need not if there is cause to believe it was being committed.

In this case it was found that the store detective had a greater authority than that of a private citizen, since she had been appointed a deputy police officer. Therefore, it was not necessary to prove an actual theft had taken place, but that probable cause was present.

FRANCIS SIMA v.
SKAGGS PAYLESS DRUG
CENTER, INC.

SUPREME COURT OF IDAHO

July 1, 1960

ON December 15, 1958 at around 6:00 P.M., Francis Sima entered Skaggs Payless Drug Store. He proceeded to a table in the rear of the store where he picked up a bar of soap and several flashlight lenses. While doing this, he was watched by a store employee named Trueworthy.

There is a difference of opinion as to what happened next. The store employee testified that Sima paid only for the soap by placing 15¢ in the checker's hand. Sima testified he paid for the lenses.

Trueworthy and another employee followed Sima outside the store and asked him if he had merchandise he had not paid for. Trueworthy testified that Sima offered them a dollar. Sima testified he made the offer of money because he thought there was some misunderstanding about the price of the articles.

Sima testified further that he was taken by the arms and returned to the store where his pockets were searched. The store employee testified that he returned voluntarily and only the bag was searched. The police arrived and Sima was taken into custody.

Sima was found not guilty of shoplifting and brought an action for false imprisonment and for false arrest.

Sima contended at the trial that in order for a citizen to make an arrest for a misdemeanor without a warrant, it must take place in his presence. Trueworthy had observed Sima's actions but two other employees who assisted Trueworthy had not. Therefore, Sima contended that as to the two other employees it was an illegal arrest. He also alleged that the search was unlawful.

The court dismissed the action. It found that Trueworthy had probable cause to make an arrest as it happened in his presence. The other employees involved merely were called upon to assist Trueworthy in the arrest. Also, a search incident to a legal arrest is not unlawful. Since the arrest was lawful the search was valid.

JOHN F. SNYDER, JR. v. COMMONWEALTH OF VIRGINIA

SUPREME COURT OF APPEALS OF VIRGINIA

September 8, 1961

JOHN Snyder was charged as an accomplice in the theft of a diamond ring. The problem presented by this case is whether the facts support the contention that Snyder took part in the theft.

On February 26, 1960 Snyder entered a jewelry store owned by Edward Foster. He engaged Foster in a conversation about a ring he had lost. After leaving the jewelry store he met two other men at a restaurant from which they went to a bar. Snyder had been acquainted with both men for several years.

Upon leaving "Billy's Beer Joint," Snyder and one of the other men named Tasker drove to the jewelry store. They entered the store together and Snyder told the owner, Foster, that he would like to look at a lady's wrist watch. He said he intended to buy the watch as a gift for his wife.

While Tasker and Snyder were looking at two watches taken from the showcase, the third man, named Brizendine, entered the store. No acknowledgement that the three men knew each other passed among them.

Foster told Brizendine he would be with him shortly, whereupon Snyder said "Go ahead and wait on him, we're in no hurry." Foster then waited on Brizendine, who said he would like to buy a ring for his wife. Foster produced a tray containing twelve rings each in a separate slot on the tray. There were no emply slots on the tray.

Brizendine examined several rings, including a $1500.00 Columbia-mounted diamond ring. The rings were returned to the tray. While Brizendine was looking at some other rings,

Snyder asked the owner a question about the watches. Foster turned and answered the question. Snyder and Tasker then left the store saying they would return later.

The store owner then returned to his one remaining customer, Brizendine. He picked out a set of rings from the second tray stating that he wanted Foster to hold them for him. He said he would bring his wife in to look at the rings he had chosen. He then left the store, about thirty seconds after Snyder had left. He immediately went to "Billy's Beer Joint" and met Snyder and Tasker after attempting to pawn the stolen ring.

Brizendine had been convicted of stealing the ring at a prior trial. The Commonwealth's case against Snyder proceeded on the theory that he aided and abetted in the theft; that he was an accomplice.

Snyder based his defense on the contention that the evidence was insufficient to support the theory that he was an accomplice. In finding Snyder guilty, the court outlined the evidence that indicated Snyder's guilt.

Mere presence at the site where a crime is committed is not enough to make a person an accomplice. One must be present and in addition invite, encourage, advise, or assist in the criminal act.

The evidence warrants the conclusion that Snyder was an accomplice. His prior trip to the store could be taken as a surveying of the scene. His meeting with Brizendine and Tasker prior to the crime as a meeting to plan its perpetration. It could be inferred that his presence at the store was to direct attention from Brizendine. The evidence shows the ring was stolen at that moment. Also the meeting after the crime could be construed as the attempt to divide the spoils.

On the facts as presented, a jury could find that Snyder was an aider and abetter in that he was present at the crime and helped in its accomplishment.

STATE v. CHARLES M. BENNETT

SUPREME COURT OF RHODE ISLAND

March 13, 1961

ON September 22, 1958 Frank Dalessio was repairing the roof of a drugstore located in a shopping center. While doing his work, he testified that he observed a green car in the parking lot. He noticed something suspicious and notified a policeman.

The police officer testified that he then placed the car under observation. He saw three men leave the car and enter a clothing store in the shopping center called Hanson's. Bennett was carrying a briefcase, and one of the other men was carrying a red wastebasket. The third man was empty-handed. A few minutes later Bennett and the man carrying the wastebasket emerged from the store. They went to the car and opened the trunk. They stood there for a couple of minutes, then closed the trunk and reentered the store. Later they again left the store, still carrying the briefcase and wastebasket and went over to the car. This time they opened a door to the car and stood there for a short period of time. He could not see what they did at the car. They then left the area of the car and began to window shop.

The police parked behind the car and took Bennett and his companion into custody. A police officer entered Hanson's and saw the third man just paying for some purchases. He was also taken into custody.

At the police station the vehicle, which was registered to Bennett was searched. Three suits were found under a blanket in the rear seat, and three suits were found under some newspapers in the trunk. The store manager was called to the station where he identified the suits as belonging to Hanson's and also stated that they had not been sold.

All three participants were convicted of larceny. They argue, however, that the only evidence against them is the possession of the stolen property and this alone is not enough to infer that they committed a larceny.

The court rejected this argument. Possession of stolen property, at least when recently after a theft, is sufficient to infer guilt of the theft when not sufficiently explained. In this case, however, the court found other evidence to justify the conviction. In addition to possession of the stolen property, the eyewitness evidence of the three men arriving together, going in and out of the store, and carrying the briefcase and basket to the trunk also constituted evidence of guilt.

The court also noted that the third participant, who actually made purchases in the store, may be held to have had constructive possession of the stolen property because he acted in concert with his co-conspirators.

STATE v. CHARLES JESSE THOMPSON

DISTRICT COURT OF APPEAL, CALIFORNIA

March 11, 1958

THIS case illustrates the necessary elements of a successful prosecution for petty theft.

On December 9, 1956 the defendant entered the Thrifty Drug Store and went to the phonograph record section. He selected seven long playing records from a display rack, and concealed them inside his coat. He started to leave the store, went through the checkstand, and was apprehended about ten feet past the checkout stand. An attempt to escape failed.

The defendant was in front of the cigarette counter when apprehended, still in a portion of the store where merchandise was available for selection and purchase.

Theft may be defined as the felonious taking of property which is not one's own. The state must prove that the thief intended to deprive the owner of his property. To accomplish this, a showing must be made that the property had been removed from the owner's possession or control, if only for one moment in time.

The court found all the elements of theft present in the evidence. The defendant concealed the records on his person, carried them past the checkout counter thereby removing them from the owner's control. The fact that the defendant was still in the store is immaterial. He cannot be relieved of his responsibility simply because his attempt to carry away the goods was frustrated. Going past the checkout counter was enough to remove the goods from the owner's control.

The most important element of theft is the showing of an intent to steal. This element can be inferred by all the evidence presented to the court or jury. Here, the concealment, the carrying through the checkout counter, and the attempted escape are sufficient evidence to infer intent.

DORCIS STIENBAUGH and JEAN ROBERTS v. PAYLESS DRUG STORE, INC.

SUPREME COURT OF NEW MEXICO

May 4, 1965

THE two customers were shopping together at a Payless Drug Store which is a self-service type store. An employee of the store saw them standing in front of a shelf. One of them picked up a box of merchandise from the shelf and removed the sticker from the box. She then placed the box in her purse.

The clerk testified that later he saw the customer open her purse to remove a cigarette and he then saw the box of merchandise in her purse. He told the store manager, who observed the customers for a few minutes, then called the police.

The police arrived and the manager pointed out the two customers who were still in the store. He told the police he suspected them of shoplifting and he suggested that they be detained and questioned, as well as searched.

The customers told the police they did examine some merchandise but that they replaced it on the shelf after examining it. After the customers were released the box of merchandise was found about fifteen feet from its original location with the price tag missing.

Both customers brought an action for false imprisonment. The issue was tried before a jury. The question to be resolved was whether the store had reasonable cause to detain and search the customers. Since the testimony was conflicting, the jury could believe either witness. The jury found against the store, apparently deciding to believe the customers' testimony. The jury also found against the store on a charge of slander. The store manager accused the customers of theft in front of witnesses, and since no reasonable cause was found, this amounted to slander.

Although the jury's verdict was for both customers, they should be distinguished in reviewing the facts. The manager was clearly wrong in accusing the customer that did not handle the merchandise. There was no evidence based on the clerk's observations that she had committed any wrongful act.

MARY SWETNAM v.
F. W. WOOLWORTH COMPANY

SUPREME COURT OF ARIZONA

November 26, 1957

AN action for false arrest and false imprisonment based on a charge by Mrs. Swetnam that she was wrongly accused of taking a scarf.

The events of this case took place in October of 1952. Mrs. Swetnam entered Woolworths carrying a scarf in her hand as well as some packages. The scarf had been a gift from her son. After entering the store she stopped at a counter containing some scarfs for sale. She put down her packages on the counter. She spent about five minutes at the counter looking at the scarfs. She then picked up her packages and walked away.

Mrs. Swetnam could not recall at this point whether she had put her scarf down with her packages, however it was in her hand as she walked away. She noticed a young man following her from the counter. She went to another counter and checked her packages. Then she had lunch in the store.

When she finished her lunch she was approached by the store manager, John Kerr. Mr. Kerr jerked the scarf out of her hand and said "Do you want this scarf?" She replied "I most certainly do. It is mine." He said "Didn't you pick that scarf up back there?" She replied "No, sir, I did not." He said "You come and go with me."

At this point Mrs. Swetnam gave two different stories of what happened next. Her first version was that she took four or five steps with Kerr and stopped. She asked where they were going and whether he was accusing her of taking the scarf. She said she then took the scarf away from him and reclaimed her packages before leaving the store.

The other version was quite similar; that she proceeded to the other side of the store with Kerr. She then stated that she had done nothing wrong and left.

False imprisonment is the direct or indirect restraint on personal liberty. The required restraint can arise from threats and need not be by actual physical force. Words alone can restrain a person's liberty. With these definitions in mind, Mrs. Swetnam's testimony should be reviewed.

No matter which version of her story is chosen, it is clear that no false imprisonment took place. In both instances Mrs. Swetnam walked away from the store manager at the point that she felt she no longer wanted to remain with him. In one version she walked a few steps, in the other she walked across the store. But in both cases she left by her own volition.

Thus her charge that she was restrained by force or fear of force is proven by her own testimony to be unfounded. Also, no threats are evident in her testimony. As a matter of fact Kerr never accused Mrs. Swetnam of stealing the scarf. When Mrs. Swetnam asked Kerr if he was accusing her of stealing the scarf, Kerr replied "Well, we have many things like that."

The court stated that had an accusation of theft taken place, it would not be evidence of false imprisonment. The words must show that a person would believe he is being restrained. Mrs. Swetnam was free to leave when she chose, and in fact did so.

HELEN N. TOCKER v.
THE GREAT ATLANTIC &
PACIFIC TEA COMPANY

DISTRICT OF COLUMBIA COURT OF APPEALS

April 22, 1963

THE customer brought an action for slander and for false arrest against the store.

She entered the store, made some purchases, and then paid for them and left. A few minutes later she returned to the store in order to make an additional purchase. She stopped in front of the cheese display after selecting the additional item. She picked up a package of cheese, walked away from the counter, and then turned around and replaced it in the display.

She paid for the additional item and left the store. The manager of the store went out the door ahead of her. He took a few steps on the sidewalk and turned around to face her.

He said "What did you do with that package of cheese you had in your hand?" She replied, "I put it right back with the other cheese — are you accusing me of taking it?"

"I have been stopping people because the other day a woman bought meat and put it in with the cereals. Did you put the cheese on the cereal counter?"

"No, I told you, if you go back and look, you will find a package of about 9¾ ounces of cheese right where I said I put it, with the other cheeses."

The first issue was whether or not the customer was slandered by this exchange. There was no obvious slander, such as accusing the customer of a crime. The court did not determine whether the store manager's words were capable of being interpreted as slanderous because it found a necessary element of slander missing.

In order for someone to be slandered, it is necessary to show that someone else overheard the slander. This is because the wrong involved is to one's reputation. There was no proof offered that others overheard the conversation. Also, no proof that the manager spoke in a loud voice. The mere fact that others were in the area is not enough to prove that the conversation was overheard.

The court could assume the exchange was overheard if other evidence had been offered; such as the loudness of the voice, the distance of the other people from the front of the store, whether they stopped to listen, etc.

The second allegation was that of false imprisonment. The term is defined as unlawful detention for any length of time, which includes deprivation of personal freedom. Here there was no showing that by words or actions the manager detained the customer. No evidence that a fear was created in the customer that the manager would use physical force to detain her. The charge was dismissed.

EPILOGUE

THE central purpose for the collection of these particular cases is to acquaint retail personnel with the legal consequences of certain acts done for security reasons.

Because of the tremendous turnover of personnel in the retail business, employees rarely have the opportunity to see the possible consequences of their initial action in regard to a security situation. Therefore, these cases have been chosen to cover various possible situations that occur frequently in a moderately sized retail business. However, fair warning must be given that the same result at trial will not follow in each situation. Not only do small variances in the facts change the result, but people themselves project a different image that alters the conclusion. In addition, the law itself is sufficiently fluid to reflect the changing moral values of the community. A recent case that is not as yet finalized so that it cannot be included in the selected cases presented, yet is complete enough to be mentioned as a possible portent of future problems in this area follows.

The shopper involved in this case was sixty-eight years old at the time of the incident, and himself the owner of a drug store. Details are sketchy at this time because the case has not been fully reported. However, the facts generally are that the shopper was shopping in another drug store. He took a package of lifesavers out of his pocket after leaving the store, and put one in his mouth.

An off-duty police officer, acting as a security guard for the drug store, asked him to return to the store. He refused at first to return, whereupon the police officer showed him his regular police badge. He then returned to the store.

At the store he told the police officer and the store manager to call his own store to verify the packages of lifesavers had been purchased there. They refused to do this, and the police officer forcibly obtained the lifesavers and requested he sign a statement admitting that the lifesavers were stolen. He refused to sign the statement and was arrested and brought to trial for larceny.

At the trial, two important items of evidence were presented. First, that the police officer had made out an arrest report stating that he witnessed the theft. The police officer admitted that this was not true. Secondly, it was shown that the packages of lifesavers had identifying lot numbers stamped on them, and that no one had bothered to check and see if these lot numbers conformed to those in stock at the store.

This case was heard in the United States District Court of California and the issue was whether the plaintiff's civil rights had been violated. The finding in this court was for the plaintiff shopper who was awarded $125,000 in punitive damages and $27,125 in compensatory damages.

The state court actions for false arrest and false imprisonment arising out of the incident were still pending at the time of this finding.

Whatever the final result in this case, it points out a new and potent source of liability for the store owner. It is more important than ever that store employees be educated to an awareness of the consequences of their behavior in this area of their duties.

INDEX